How to Make a Free W...

For Kids

Entrepreneur Book Series

M. Usman

Mendon Cottage Books

JD-Biz Publishing

Our books are available at
1. Amazon.com
2. Barnes and Noble
3. Itunes
4. Kobo
5. Smashwords
6. Google Play Books

Table of Contents

Preface

If you have always wanted to have a website, there is no better time to achieve your dream than now. Due to advancements in web designing, you do not need to spend years learning HTML; "drag and drop" website builders make everything easy for newbies. Sweetening the deal even further, you can create your website without spending a penny.

However, the difficult part is finding a good provider that will let you make a decent free website. As you may know, "free" usually comes at a cost. In this book, not only will I show you how to create a website, but I will also recommend some of the best free website providers you can sign up with.

Anyone who has ever started a website knows that making it is easy. But, finding motivation to keep it going is the most difficult part. So, I will also give you tips you can follow to keep on creating content. Furthermore, there are sections in the book dealing with website promotion, SEO, and other topics.

Since the internet can be dangerous to young people, I recommend that you communicate to your parents or guardians about your intentions to make a free website. It's even better if they take part in the whole process.

So without further ado, let's get started.

Chapter # 1: Benefits of Having a Website

Years ago, a website was a luxury only affordable to big companies. But today, anyone can have it in minutes, and sometimes, without spending any money. The world is changing; it's either you change with it or get left behind.

In this chapter, I will show you some of the benefits you will enjoy from having a website of your own.

Share Your Ideas – Your website will give you a platform to share your ideas with the world. You may be surprised to find how many people will be inspired by your words. These could be fellow kids or even adults.

Your ideas do not need to be extraordinary. You can share jokes you have been working on, cool inventions you recently discovered, stories, etc.

Showcase Your Skills – If you are good at drawing and believe that you can touch someone with your art, then get a free website. If you write stories you would love to share with fellow kids, then you definitely need to have a website. In fact, whatever your art, a website is the best place to present it to the whole world.

Even better, a website will force you to only create the best content. In the end, your work will improve and your website will become popular.

You Will Learn to be Social – Humans are social animals and cannot exist in a vacuum. However, learning to interact with others is not easy. But when you have a website, you will build relationships with your visitors.

Although some of these friends will go, some will stay. And with time, you will discover that your communication skills are improving. Striking conversations with strangers will become easy. And this is a skill everyone needs in life. You will use it at work when you grow up, at school, etc.

Understand the World – The internet connects people from every corner of the globe. As long as you do not live in the middle of nowhere, you can get online and enjoy some of the things the web has to offer. For you, this is a chance to reach people from all walks of life. By interacting with them, you will learn how the world works.

You Will Become Familiar with the Web – Almost everything can now be done on the web. So, by having your own website, you will learn how the internet works. The best part is that you will do this without the pressure of wanting to master everything because you are still young. By the time you are matured, establishing successful websites will be in your blood and you will not waste time learning new things.

Since we are only focusing on free websites in this book, you will not waste any money in the process. You can make as many websites as you need; if you know you can manage them, your imagination is the limit.

Chapter # 2: Signing Up for a Website in Weebly

Weebly is one of the oldest website builders on the internet. Once you register for a free account, you are given all the tools you may need to have a complete and professional website. If your needs outgrow the free plan, you can upgrade to any of the paying packages.

Making Weebly even better is that it is very affordable. Furthermore, the team behind it constantly adds features to the platform.

Before we go on to look at how you can create a website in Weebly, let's look at why you should choose it.

Drag and Drop Website Builder – If you have limited knowledge on web designing, there is no need to worry. With Weebly's website builder, you can drag any element in order to make the website look the way you want.

Great Pricing – As I said in the introduction, Weebly is affordable. If you decide to go for the paying plans, you will find Weebly cheaper than other websites.

Lots of Features – Weebly has a number of features that will allow you to create a professional website and let it grow. However, there are still other features we would like to see added.

The biggest downside with Weebly is that if you decide to move to another platform, the process is one big headache. It is very technical and time-consuming, and you will likely give up before you even start.

How to Create a Website in Weebly

Creating a website in Weebly is very easy. Here are the steps you must follow:

1. Go to Weebly's website by typing www.weebly.com in your web browser's address bar.

2. You will be presented with a page to fill in your name, email address, and password after which you select "Get Started."

3. On the next page, choose whether you are making a site, blog, or store.

4. Select a theme from those available. You must choose one that is close to what you are looking for.

5. You will then need to select a name for your website. Remember to keep it short, meaningful, and easy to remember. And since this is a free website, know that it will be www.yourname.weebly.com (not bad for a free website).

6. You website is now almost done. Use the drag and drop editor to move things around. Although you have freedom to do whatever you want here, I

would recommend that you do not overdo it.

7. Hit the "Publish" button and your website will be online. You can start adding text, pictures, and anything else you want.

Understand that it will take time to get used to working in Weebly. So for a start, take time to familiarize yourself with it. You will find that it pays in the long run to do so. There are instructional videos and articles on the net you can use to speed up the learning process.

For your own safety, make sure you are working with an adult during this process.

Chapter # 3: Creating a Free Website in Wix

Wix's characteristics resemble those of Weebly, although the two are not a copy of one another. When you register with Wix, you will get all the tools you need to make your website grow for free. However, if you want to make a professional impression, it is recommended that you upgrade to any of the paying plans, which are affordable.

Here are some of the reasons to choose Wix:

Drag and Drop Website Builder – Just like with Weebly, you will find a drag and drop website builder in Wix. Personally, I prefer Wix's builder over the one in Weebly. However, both of these are easy to use and very functional, so do not let this be a deciding factor.

Beautiful Templates – Wix has a number of beautiful templates. So, not only will your website look elegant, but it will also look professional. Making it even better, you can rearrange any element with the builder to make your website look unique.

Free Space – Since you will need space to keep all your content, Wix will give you 500mb of storage when you register. Unless you will be uploading videos, this is enough for standard pictures and texts. And if you ever run out of space, you can easily upgrade to another plan.

The only thing I do not like about Wix's free plan is that you will have Wix ads on your website, which can take away your readers attention. However, know that it is not easy to find a decent free plan that won't want to put advertisements on your website.

How to Sign Up for a Free Website

Here the steps you must follow when you want to get a Wix website:

1. Go to Wix's home page by typing www.wix.com in your web browser.

2. Click the "Start Now" button and a pop-up will appear.

3. Select "I'm a new user" and hit the "Go" button.

4. You will land on a new page where you will have to provide your email address and create a password to proceed. If you do not have an email address, you can involve your parents or guardian

5. You will then need to select a category which relates to your topic. It helps to understand what your website is all about before you even go to Wix's home page.

6. The next page will give you an option to select a template. You must be careful, because once you make your choice, you will not have the freedom to

change to another template.

7. When done, click "Edit" to change any aspects you do not like about the template. As always, it is a good idea not to overdo it. Just a little goes a long way in making the difference you want.

8. Click "Save" and name your website.

9. You can now hit the "Publish" button to make your website visible to the whole world. If you already have some content, you can post it to familiarize yourself with how Wix works.

Chapter # 4: Creating a WordPress Website

I personally love using WordPress because of its robust features and ease of use. WordPress has been around for a long time and it's no coincidence that it now powers over 20% of the websites on the internet. More people are still joining its bandwagon, so that percentage is expected to rise.

Here are some of the reasons you may want to use WordPress:

Lots of Themes – If you want your website to have a specific look, you will easily get what you want with WordPress, as there are lots of themes for you to choose from. Some of these require that you pay while others are totally free. However, having lots of themes means you may be overwhelmed and not know which one to choose.

Customization – Although there is no drag and drop website builder in WordPress, it is still one of the most highly customizable platforms in existence. Once you choose a theme, you have the freedom to change its appearance as much as you want.

Lots of Plugins – If there is something you need that your theme does not provide, you can easily fulfill that need with a plugin. For example, many themes do not include a contact form, but you can get this by installing a plugin.

However, since there are a lot of features in WordPress, you will need to take time learning your way around. Additionally, if you choose the free plan, you will get a long address in the form of www.yourname.wordpress.com.

Creating a Website

Here are the steps you must follow:

1. Go to www.wordpress.com in your browser.

2. Click the "Create Website" button.

3. You will land on a page with a number of themes. Go through these and choose the one you think will be the best for your website (note that you can switch to another theme at any time from the dashboard).

4. Next, you will need to create a domain name. Since you are creating a free website, you will need to go with the free domain name. Play with a couple of words because what you want may already be taken. As you do this, remember to keep the name meaningful and easy to remember.

5. When done, you will then be presented with a page to select a plan. Again, you will need to go for the free plan.

6. Now you will need to fill all the necessary information, after which an activation email will be sent to the email address you provided. To access this

email, login to your mailbox and follow the instructions in the email.

Once you are done verifying, your website will be ready. You can start posting whatever it is you have always wanted to share with the world. Take time to familiarize yourself with WordPress; it is a lot of work, but worth the effort. You can change the look of your site by clicking the appearance tab in dashboard.

Chapter # 5: Introduction to SEO

If you want to get a lot of visitors from Google and other search engines, you must make sure that your website is optimized.

SEO stands for Search Engine Optimization. In essence, it is a process of making your website get discovered by search engines. It includes the use of texts, images, linking, etc.

Considering how complex this topic is, I would recommend that you work with an adult. They will help you understand it and also lend a hand with issues like keyword research, backlinking, and more.

Why do SEO

You may wonder why on earth anyone should be bothered with SEO. Here are some of the reasons:

Get Free Visitors – When your website is optimized for search engines, it will be displayed on the first page of search results. It is not customary of internet users to go through a series of pages; they usually click what's on the first page. So if you can optimize your website to rank highly, you will get a lot of free visitors.

You Will Strive to Produce Great Content – Websites that are ranked highly in search results are always popular and this is not a coincidence. Search engines love great content. So in an effort to improve your rank, you will also improve your content.

Improves Your Website's Friendliness – There are a lot of factors that are taken into account before determining your rank. Quick load times and navigability are among these. And these are also the same factors that will make your website be friendly to humans.

How to do Basic SEO

Start With Keywords

Keywords refer to a group of words people use when searching for something on the internet. For example, "how to make a free website" is a keyword. So the question is… Where do you get these words?

There are a lot of keyword tools on the internet, but for simplicity, you can use Google's keyword research tool. The best part is that it has everything you need, and at the same time, it is free. All you need to do is log in with your Google account and start searching.

You must find words that have a lot of monthly searches to get more traffic to your website.

Using Keywords

Once you have found a keyword, you will need to use it when writing your posts and in your images.

Start with the heading. If the keyword is "free website", you can have "How to Make a Free Website" or "Free Website Builders" as the title. Since the heading is what search engines will look at first, you must ensure that the keyword is woven into it.

The keyword must also be placed in any subheadings that you have.

After the headings, you must ensure that the rest of the body also has the keyword. Most importantly, you must have it in the first and last paragraphs as these are places search spiders do not miss.

Take caution to avoid using the keyword too much or you will be penalized for keyword stuffing.

If you have images in the post, make sure that they also have the keyword in the Alt tag. Search engines will read this to tell what the image is all about, as they do not have eyes to see it.

Another SEO technique you must practice is linking your posts to each other on your website. As you do this, place the keyword in the hyperlink.

However, you must remember one thing when you are writing your posts— you are creating content for humans and not search engines. So do not force the keyword into the post, let it happen naturally.

Chapter # 6: Things to Keep in Mind When Creating Content

While you are free to have anything you want on your website, you must ensure that you are only creating content that will not land you into trouble. Otherwise, in most cases, the worst you will get is having your website deleted meaning you will lose all your work in an instant.

I would recommend that you read the terms and conditions before creating your website. Working with an adult at this stage is beneficial, as they will help interpret some of the things beyond your understanding.

Here are some things you must remember:

Create Your Own Content – Since this is probably your first website, you may not be good at making your content. So you may be tempted to do what many new website owners do—copy content from other websites.

However, this practice is unprofessional so you must avoid it. If you are not good at writing, simply work on it. With time, you will get better. There are no shortcuts here but to work until you become perfect. You may involve an adult in the process to help with content creation and show you how it's done.

Be Careful With Images – If you want to add images on your website, make sure that you have the authorization to do so. Simply getting images from Google and posting them on your website will bring you problems you are not yet ready to handle. For all you know, most of the images you will get from Google are copyright protected.

My advice is that you should make your own images. If you can't, you can use websites that provide free images like pixabay.com, freephotosbank.com, and morguefile.com. It is better to be safe than sorry.

Have a Main Topic – You are free to develop a website that covers everything under the sun. However, it helps to have a single topic that you will be writing about. This will make it easy for search engines to understand what your website is all about.

Additionally, your visitors will know what to expect every time they visit it. Furthermore, you will find it easy to keep coming up with content because you will have a better understanding of your topic.

Avoid Content that Can Lead to Violence – When you are creating your posts, images, or anything, you should make sure that you do not offend anyone. Otherwise, people will hate you and everything you represent. You will lose readers which will ultimately lead to the fall of your website.

The type of content you must avoid is one that insults other people's religions, race, political affiliations, etc.

Adding to that, you must avoid using words that might be seen as offensive.

Besides, as a kid, you are not even supposed to be using such words.

Websites are made of content. Follow these tips and you will have content that people want to read. The trick is to work as hard as you can and you will see a boost in traffic.

Chapter # 7: Promoting Your Website

If no one knows about your website, no matter how great it is, you can forget about the possibility of seeing success. Great content and a lot of visitors are what make websites become successful.

You must use proven steps to promote your website. That will enable it to rise among other websites trying to succeed.

However, the painful truth is that promoting a website is not easy or fun. It takes time and a lot of hard work to start reaping the fruits of your labor.

Below are some of the things you can do to make your website popular.

1. Use SEO

By far, optimizing your website for search engines is the best way to increase your traffic. Like stated earlier, SEO makes it possible for your website to rank highly in search results, meaning you get lots of free visitors. I am sure you are familiar with the basics of SEO from Chapter 5.

2. Use Social Media

In any promotional campaign you can carry for your website, you must ensure that social media is included. This means using websites like Facebook, Pinterest, Google+, Twitter, YouTube, etc. But like with everything, being successful with social media demands that you work hard at it. You will also need to have a lot of fans which will lead to more visitors to your website.

3. Write Content for Other Websites

I would only recommend that you start creating articles for other websites when you perfect your writing skills. Otherwise, you will find it hard to get your articles accepted which will kill your motivation. You must focus on submitting them to websites that are already ranking highly in Search results. Since a link to your website will be included in the article, you will get quality backlinks which will be beneficial to your SEO efforts.

For a start, you can try writing for Hubpages, Ezine articles, and similar sites. However, the links you will get from these are not of high quality. So do not expect to see miracles in your traffic. But a low quality backlink is better than having no link.

4. Join Forums

If you can manage to find a forum that is related to the topic your website is covering, join it and post links to your website. Be careful to not overdo it or you will be labeled as a spammer and face the termination of your account.

5. Ask Visitors to Do Things for You

Sometimes, people want to be told what to do. So if you have a considerable number of visitors, you can ask them to share your content with their friends, bookmark your website, comment on your post, etc.

You must try to interact with your visitors all the time. If someone leaves a comment, even replying with a "thank you" goes a long way. If someone writes something that offends you, simply delete their comment. You must not respond rudely to anyone no matter how much they upset you.

Chapter # 8: How to Be Safe Online

It is no secret that the internet has made life better. But at the same time, we must also acknowledge that it has created problems. Online theft, human trafficking, cyberbullying, pornography, and other issues are on the rise.

Unfortunately, it's kids who face the highest risk, as they are easy to manipulate. But with a few tips, any child can resist these dangers and still enjoy the benefits of having an online presence.

1. Involve an Adult in Everything You Do Online

Although I have been saying this throughout the book, I believe it deserves another mention here. As you are making your website, make sure there is an adult involved in the process. Not only will they help in creating your website and making content for it, but they will also keep you safe when online.

2. Keep Personal Information to Yourself

Any information that may be used to identify you must not be shared with strangers. This includes email address, phone number, location, home address, etc.

Before you submit personal information when creating an online account, make sure that the website is secure. If you are not sure, ask an adult to help you figure it out.

3. Post Your Images Online Carefully

Once you have posted an image online, know that it is up for grabs. Anyone can do as they wish with it and there is nothing you can do about it. So if you are planning on sharing your images online, think if it is worth the risk.

4. Don't Share Passwords and Usernames

If someone with bad intentions gets his hands on your password and username, know that they have the keys to access your private information. To avoid this, never share passwords or usernames with anyone else but your parents.

It is a bad idea to write these down as someone can easily gain access to them. If you are afraid that you will forget, there are a lot of tools that will keep all your passwords and usernames safe.

For increased security, change your password every 3 months.

5. Exercise Caution with People You Meet Online

You will certainly make new friends online by having your own website.

However, if anyone asks for something that makes you uncomfortable, get your defenses up. For example, if someone requests that you should meet, talk to your parents. If they say it's all right to meet that person, let them come with you.

6. Don't Respond to Rude Messages

If someone sends you a message that upsets you or makes you uncomfortable, do not respond. Simply block that person to keep him from sending more messages. Additionally, you must remember to tell your parents about it.

7. Don't Just Install Software

If you have software you would like to install on your computer, be sure that the software is safe. You can achieve this by only getting your software from trusted sources. Furthermore, you can ask an adult to help you with this as well.

Chapter # 9: Finding Motivation

Creating a website is easy. The difficult part is coming up with content to keep it going. And as you may know by now, it is content that makes or breaks a website.

In this chapter, I will give you tips that will help you keep on creating content, even when you have lost your motivation.

If you are serious about success, you should ensure that you are updating your website at least twice per week.

1. Have a goal – It is important to have a good reason for taking a specific course of action. If you do not, you will likely lose your motivation. The same is true when you are making a website. You need to be clear about what it is you want to achieve. It could be that you want to help people find ways of making money online or you have skills that you want the world to discover. Whatever the reason, write it down and look at it from time to time.

2. Make a website about something you love – People usually lose motivation to keep updating their websites when creating content becomes a chore. To avoid that from happening, make a website about a topic you love. If you love writing stories, make a website centered on that. If you are into computers, do not be intimidated by the uncountable number of computer websites on the net. You can create your content from a new angle, setting your website apart.

3. Set time – You could say every day before going to school, you will have 30 minutes just for creating content for you website. With time, this will become a habit and you will find it easy to work every day.

4. Break things – Writing can sometimes be a daunting task. Thinking "I must finish a 500-word article" when all you have is a heading, will surely lead to a loss of motivation. Instead, break your task into smaller chunks. First go do your research and then make an outline of what you are going to write. You will discover that it becomes easier that way. You must also remember to plan for any notes that will be useful in your post.

5. Write every day – By doing this, you will make writing become part of you. With time, it will start feeling natural, so you will never need motivation to get started. Some say you must do something 27 times to make it a habit. But this is not necessarily so. You just need to keep doing it for as long as it takes till it becomes a habit.

6. Reward yourself – This is probably the one thing you must do every time you need to motivate yourself. When you want to write, set some kind of a reward and give it to yourself if you manage to write what you wanted to.

Conclusion

Having reached this far, I would like to thank you for reading the book. I am sure it has helped you discover how you can make a free website, even as a kid. Once your website is online, remember to keep adding great content to it. It's a lot of work, but worth the effort in the end.

If you see that your needs have outgrown the free plan, you are free to upgrade. So before making your choice as to which free website provider to go for, ensure that your selection has all the needs you will want in future. Visit all the websites I gave in the book to review their plans and features. Moving a website or upgrading to another plan can be a cause of a stinging headache if you do not make the right decision at this stage.

There are a lot of benefits you will get for having your own website, but most importantly, you will share your knowledge with the world and also learn a lot of things in the process.

Once your website is online, you have reached the point of no return. So keep working hard and success will come your way.

Reference Images

https://pixabay.com/en/children-win-success-video-game-593313/

https://pixabay.com/en/boy-girl-children-computer-110762/

https://pixabay.com/en/notebook-technology-keyboard-laptop-791292/

https://pixabay.com/en/blogging-computer-female-girl-15968/

https://pixabay.com/en/wordpress-hand-logo-589121/

https://pixabay.com/en/seo-sem-marketing-optimization-758264/

https://pixabay.com/en/mac-freelancer-macintosh-macbook-459196/

https://pixabay.com/en/social-media-twitter-facebook-763731/

https://pixabay.com/en/boy-face-think-laptop-blue-713273/

https://pixabay.com/en/laptop-human-hands-keyboard-typing-820274/

Author Bio

Muhammad Usman is a distinguished medical graduate of Allama Iqbal medical college (AIMC). He is a professional writer who has been in the field for more than 4 years. During this time he has produced 10,000+ articles, blogs, and eBooks on various niches related to diseases, health, fitness, nutrition, and well-being. He is a regular contributor to several journals related to medicine and surgery. He is the editor of several journals and newspapers.

Download Free Books!

http://MendonCottageBooks.com

Check out some of the other JD-Biz Publishing books

Gardening Series on Amazon

Health Learning Series

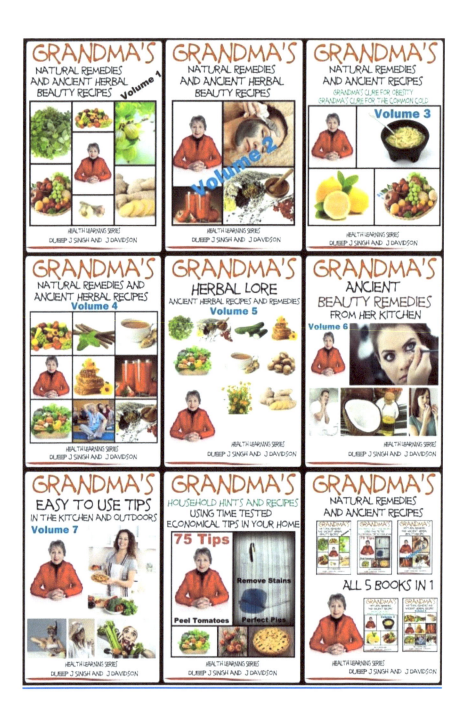

Country Life Books

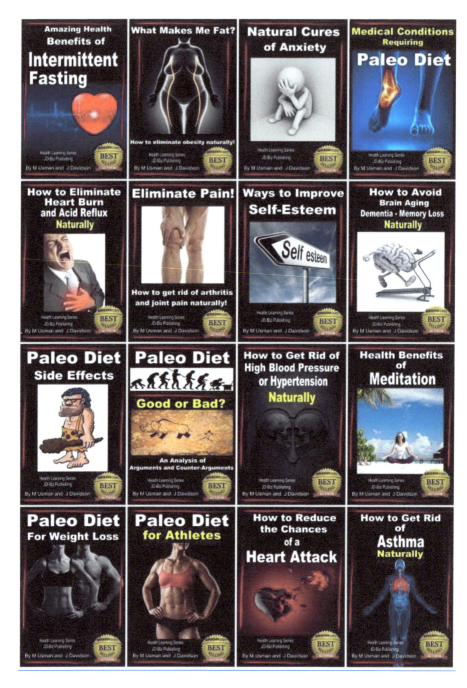

Amazing Animal Book Series

Learn To Draw Series

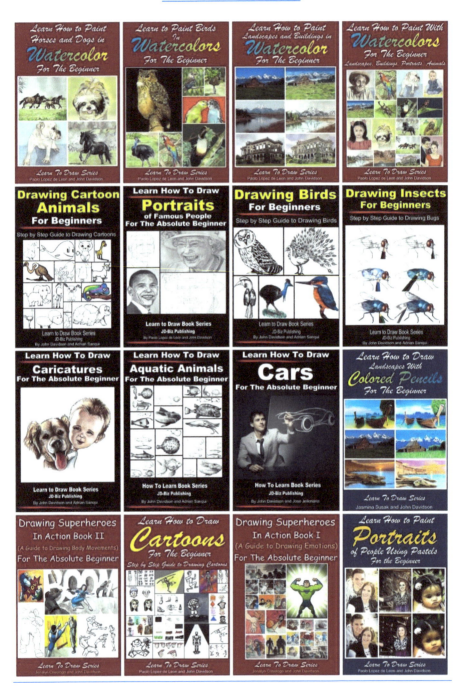

How to Build and Plan Books

Entrepreneur Book Series

Our books are available at

1. Amazon.com

2. Barnes and Noble

3. Itunes

4. Kobo

5. Smashwords

6. Google Play Books

Download Free Books!

http://MendonCottageBooks.com

Publisher

JD-Biz Corp

P O Box 374

Mendon, Utah 84325

http://www.jd-biz.com/

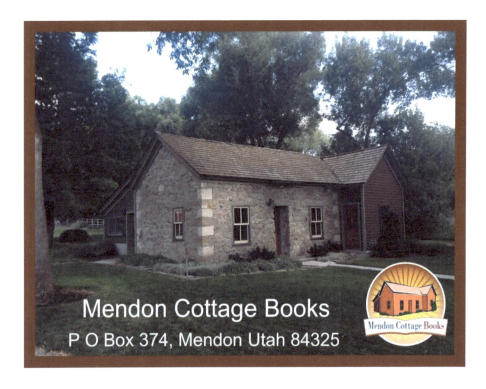

Mendon Cottage Books

P O Box 374, Mendon Utah 84325

www.ingramcontent.com/pod-product-compliance
Lightning Source LLC
Chambersburg PA
CBHW041147050326
40689CB00001B/514